Beyond the Big C

Hope in the face of death

Jeremy Marshall

10 Publishing

a division of 10ofthose.com

Beyond the Big C

Copyright © 2019 by Jeremy Marshall

First published in Great Britain in 2019

British Library Cataloguing in Publication Data

A record for this book is available from the British Library

ISBN: 978-1-913278-03-8

Designed and typeset by Jude May (judemaydesign.com)

Printed in Denmark by Nørhaven

10Publishing, a division of 10ofthose.com
Unit C, Tomlinson Road, Leyland, PR25 2DY, England

Email: info@10ofthose.com

Website: www.10ofthose.com

1 3 5 7 10 8 6 4 2

Beyond the Big C

This is the story of my journey with cancer – but, as you'll discover if you read on, it is not just about me. I am 56 years old and have had cancer for the last seven years. I want to share my experience in the hope that it helps you. As it's my story, some parts of it may be relevant to your experience, other parts may not. You can be the judge.

I am not a cancer specialist, nor am I an expert on living with cancer. This is not a book about how to cope with cancer, nor how to beat it. I don't want you to think that I am some amazing person – because I am not. Although I am a Christian, I am not an inherently 'religious' person who sails effortlessly from one high point to another. I have doubts and I am often afraid. There is nothing exceptional about me and I am very far from being a model for others. So why am I writing this short book?

I would like to introduce you to someone else – someone who has utterly transformed my life and someone without whom I couldn't survive a single day in this messed-up world.

Having incurable cancer seems a dead end. But I believe there is hope beyond the Big C.

Finding a lump

My journey began one day in early September 2012, in the shower. I felt a very small lump on my ribs. It was about the size of a couple of very small peas, buried just below the skin. I didn't think it was cancer – although, inevitably, the thought did flash through my mind. I said firmly to myself, 'Don't be ridiculous Jeremy. It's just a lump.' In fact, being a typical man, I didn't really do anything much about it for a couple of weeks until my wife Jeanette finally told me firmly, 'Go and see the GP.' So eventually, I did. The GP examined it and, to my relief, said, 'It's nothing to worry about. It's almost certainly just a fatty lump which is typical at your age (I was 49 at the time) but we will get it checked out, just to put your mind at rest.'

From there, I was referred to specialist after specialist, who all ran tests and looked puzzled. One said, 'I don't know what that is, but it is not a fatty lump.' Eventually, the doctors decided to take it out to enable a biopsy and better analysis, so I had an operation just before Christmas 2012 to remove it.

Waiting for the results

It was quite difficult to get the results back from

the local hospital after Christmas as everything was closed and then the surgeon was on holiday. Finally, after various phone calls, I started impatiently pushing the surgeon's medical secretary for an answer.

She demurred but eventually said, 'OK, well, we've referred you to the Marsden.' Everyone knows that the Royal Marsden only treats one disease – cancer. A couple of weeks later (and further multiple telephone calls from me), I got a call from the medical secretary telling me that the diagnosis was confirmed. It was a type of sarcoma and I was to see the specialist sarcoma oncologist at the Marsden the following week. That's when I first felt real terror. I felt my knees go weak and a cold hand gripping my heart.

I can still remember exactly where I was when I got the call (just north of Oxford Street on my way to a charity dinner). And how I felt – which was as if I had been punched in the face. It was hard not to let my legs buckle. I went ahead with the dinner as I thought it was too late to pull out – but, of course, my mind was fixed on the diagnosis not the dinner. On my way home, I made the terrible mistake of googling the exact type of cancer. Again, I can remember exactly where I was standing in

Waterloo station (Platform C, since you ask) and my feelings of terror when I read on my phone the very gloomy prognosis. (That is why the first thing the doctor tells you when you meet them is, 'Don't research the prognosis on the Internet!')

Meeting the specialist

When I eventually met a specialist at the Royal Marsden, he told me that I had a rare type of sarcoma which is a cancer of the muscle tissue. To be exact, a pleomorphic liposarcoma. But, good news, they had caught it early and the prognosis was fairly good: only about 20% of people had a recurrence – although, if it did recur, the prognosis was very poor. '1 in 5 – that's pretty good odds,' I thought. Being an optimistic person, I was sure I would be in the 80%. To make sure they had got all the cancerous tissue ('clearing the margins', I think it's called), I had another operation and then a course of radiotherapy which, while tiring, was tolerable. I went every day for about six weeks and lay still without moving while the machine read the tattoo marks they had placed on my body. At its worse, it felt like a mild sunburn. Apart from a few weeks to recover from the operation, I carried on working as normal, just coming in late and leaving early. Life gradually returned to normal.

Back to normal?

Everything seemed to go back to as it was. I went every three months for a check-up at the Marsden. Everything seemed fine. In fact, at the last check-up in April 2015, the specialist congratulated me on having gone two years cancer-free and that the next check-up could be in six months' time. I can remember how happy and relaxed I felt leaving the hospital. Each time after the tests, I eagerly phoned and messaged family and friends and told them: 'all good'.

Then one hot Saturday at the end of May 2015, my wife Jeanette and I were invited to dinner with some friends in Sevenoaks where we live. My whole life was about to change irretrievably. As we started dinner, I adjusted the collar on my polo shirt, which was slightly rucked. As I did that I felt a really large lump on my left collar bone. It was much larger than the pea before, more like a golf ball. I knew immediately what it was. The cancer was back. I made an excuse, went to the bathroom and examined it carefully. I felt sick to my stomach. In inner turmoil.

Not wanting to upset anyone, I went back and told my hosts, 'I'm sorry – I feel ill, I need to go home.' On the way home, I told Jeanette and, on the Monday, I arranged to go in for a scan at the Marsden on the following Friday. I would get the results in a week, on a day which is seared into my memory: Friday 13 June 2015.

Back at the Marsden

That Friday, I sat with Jeanette in the waiting room of the Marsden. As normal, the nurse came to collect us and take us through to see the oncologist. On the way, she said simply, 'I'm really sorry.' That was enough warning. My worst fears were confirmed when I entered the room. Normally, I would meet with the oncologist and a nurse. But, instead, at least half a dozen people were waiting for us.

Straightaway, they told me, 'We're really sorry: you've got five large tumours in various places throughout your body and we can't operate on them. In fact, your cancer is incurable.' The next question from me was obvious: 'What's the prognosis?' After the usual qualifications about 'difficult to say', the answer was quite bald: 18 months.

I am not ashamed to say that I burst into tears. Life changed forever.

Four years on

Now, as I write this – getting on for four years later, the situation is pretty much the same. I still have five fairly large tumours and my outlook is still as uncertain – but I'm alive! I'm incredibly grateful for the expertise of the oncologists and staff at the Marsden, plus the research on mine and other rare conditions next door at the Institute of Cancer Research. In the meantime, we've tried various experiments which haven't worked and therefore, I have basically stuck to chemotherapy.

After a while, the oncologists decided that it was not the same cancer as before but a completely different type: extrapulmonary small cell carcinoma. Quite how I got from a sarcoma to non-pulmonary small cell lung cancer and how the growths were missed after the first one, I don't know. I quite enjoy baffling the medical establishment. A specialist who saw me told me, 'You have some of the strangest symptoms I've ever seen', which I secretly enjoyed hearing.

In the meantime, I have been through four complete chemotherapy cycles, lasting about five months each. Each cycle consists of six separate treatments which take place every three weeks or so. After each, I get some time off to recover from the chemo and then we start again. It's a real pity cancer hospitals don't give 'frequent flyer' points.

Another complication

Just to add to the fun, I've had serious problems with my eyes. In 2015, at the end of the first round of chemotherapy, Jeanette and I decided to go on a 'holiday of a lifetime' to Ecuador and the Galapagos with some friends. But we never made it. On the flight on the way there, the retina in my left eye detached.

It wasn't until we were deep in the Ecuadorian rainforest that I realised what had happened. By the time we got back to Quito to have the diagnosis confirmed, it was too late to fix it. I eventually made my way back to England and was referred to St Thomas' Hospital in London where another excellent doctor put me through multiple operations – but without being able to restore sight in the left eye. However, he checked me out carefully and said that the other eye – the right one – was fine, and that lots of people only have one eye.

And another

A few months later, my right eye went in exactly the same way. This time, I was in Newbury, not Ecuador. I knew immediately what I had to do and this time, after more operations, the eye was eventually fixed. Being treated for a detached retina is an unusual experience. After the operation, you have to position your head upside down, like a bat, for 45 minutes in every 60. This goes on for a week and it enables the gas to be correctly positioned to heal the damage.

For a while, after the second operation, I was nearly blind and I had to be led around by the arm by my human guide dogs, such as my wife, children or, sometimes, one of my sisters. One of them (tongue in cheek, I hope) agreed to guide me around London holding my arm, but only on condition I wore a badge saying, 'I'm her brother, not her husband'. Charming!

Things could be a lot worse

I am acutely conscious that most people's experiences of cancer are far worse than mine. From the five tumours I have so far – even though some of them are fairly large – I have never felt anything in terms of side effects from the tumours themselves. My reaction to chemotherapy has been relatively mild compared to most people's, possibly because I have a very fast metabolism. I feel very tired and my hair falls out – which for a guy is not so bad anyway – but, after treatment, the hair has regrown and the tiredness has worn off. So far, I have never once felt sick or nauseous, for example, which is a very common side effect for many people.

I am also aware that I have many significant advantages humanly speaking – a loving family, wonderful healthcare under an excellent oncologist and eye surgeon and, perhaps most importantly, a relatively successful and, in some ways, 'moderate' treatment so far.

Really testing circumstances
I remember a friend in our church who was so badly affected by chemotherapy that she said she would rather die than have more. Tragically, that's what eventually happened: with her Christian faith undimmed and a shining example to me. I have never felt anything like that so far and I realise this is a massive advantage.

When I compare my experiences with some friends of mine in Serbia, for example, I can see that I have experienced absolutely nothing. A friend's grandson there had acute leukaemia. The treatment available in Serbia was very limited and, several times, I and others helped to send him to Italy for treatment. This helped – but eventually, he of course had to return to Serbia.

The major problem was that the general supply of drugs in Serbia – and the supply of the particular one that the boy needed – was very unreliable. Often the critical medicine was unavailable. Eventually, in desperation and with the help of a friendly doctor in the UK, we got the drug couriered to Vienna and a family member picked it up and drove it back to Serbia. Sadly, in the end, all of this was to no avail and he passed away on the day of his tenth birthday. All in all, if I compare myself with many people in the UK and elsewhere, I realise that I am truly blessed with the care I receive.

Fear

I want to be very open that I am afraid, sometimes very afraid. This is despite having a strong Christian faith. In fact, I would say that the dominant emotion I have felt since being diagnosed is fear. Fear of dying and, in particular, fear of the process leading up to death.

I have been to visit quite a number of friends and family members in the last stages of cancer and it's horrible.

Visiting loved ones and friends in hospices is a very solemn occasion. You feel overwhelmed with sorrow and compassion for them. But also somehow hopeless to do anything.

I remember one friend from work, Steve, who was in a hospice with a brain tumour. When we and other friends visited him the last time, he was unconscious. His head was swollen due to the growth of the tumours. Various other hospice visits come to mind – in particular, visiting my mother-in-law in her last few weeks. Of course, at the time, I felt very sorry for the person I was visiting – but, let's be honest, I also thought selfishly, 'Thank God it's not me'. Now when I recall those visits, I think to myself, 'Well, Jeremy, one day that will be you.'

Growing fear

Each time I had a scan or a test after the initial diagnosis, my fear grew slightly even as I hoped and anticipated getting the 'nothing to worry about' message confirmed. My fear started as a small nagging doubt. It grew silently. Each time,

I felt it slightly more strongly until, in the end, it became full-grown terror.

The whole process of diagnosis and treatment adds to this cold feeling of doubt metamorphosing into full fear. I can remember, for example, going for an MRI as part of the original diagnosis in 2012. Of all the hundreds of tests and scans I have had, I found the MRI the most unpleasant. I was wedged into what – dare I say it – feels like a coffin for about 45 minutes. The machine makes strange grinding noises as it does its business. I didn't mind the noises and you can listen to music as you lie there unmoving, with periodic instructions to hold your breath, breathe out and so on. The sensation that made me afraid was the feeling of being enclosed, of being trapped. Even – to put it melodramatically – of being buried alive. Eventually, the process was finished – and one of the happiest experiences in cancer is the feeling when your treatment finishes.

All this time, there was that tiny cold feeling of, first of all, concern; then anxiety; finally, of all-out fear, which grows and, like an invader, takes over more and more of my waking hours.

All-consuming

It became the first thing I'd think about when I woke up in the morning – 'Oh, I've got cancer.' Each time I spoke to a specialist or a doctor, I thought, 'Now I will reach the conclusion – which, I assume and hope, is an all clear.'

To start with, I thought, 'It's 99% likely to be that favourable outcome.' Then it was 95%. And then, little by little, each test put the probability a little lower. As the probability reduced, the fear inexorably and slowly grew. And all of this silent growth taking you over is, ironically, a bit like a tumour.

My 'fear index' has gone up and down over the last few years. The times I feel most acutely afraid are sitting in the waiting room, waiting for the oncologist to tell me the results of the latest scan. There's even a name for this: 'scanxiety'.

An answer to fear?

What have I found to be the answer to my fear? Fear not just of cancer but, most of all, of death. I don't see an answer to my fear if I look at the world around me. Nor do I find one if I look within.

But as I said at the beginning, this book isn't just about me – it's also about someone else. And that 'someone' does have an answer to my fear. That 'someone' is Jesus Christ. Jesus Christ, whom I believe walked the dusty roads of Palestine 2,000 years ago – and whom, I believe, you and I can know today.

Being a Christian is not about doing your best, or never doing anyone any wrong. Nor is it about being 'religious' or going to church. Being a Christian is about knowing and being known by the God who made the entire universe, whom I believe holds every atom of the universe in his control, including the atoms that make up my tumours. If you are tempted at this point to stop reading and throw the book away; please don't.

Is it true?

Consider this: if what I am saying is true, these short pages contain the answer to cancer, death and everything. If what I say is not true, you might have wasted 30 more minutes reading on from now. What do you have to lose? I am a Christian not because it's helpful (although it is) – but because it is true. I believe it's true because, when I look at the evidence, I am convinced of its claims. In many ways, its claims are preposterous, bordering on insane. For example: the claim that the maker of the universe, who created space and time, became human in the form of a few cells in the womb of a young woman in an obscure corner of the first-century Roman empire. Is that true? That's the question. My experience is that the Bible is a letter to me from the God who made the universe. And it can be the same for you. And that letter brings news of hope beyond the Big C.

A first-hand account
One of the most common commands in the Bible in general – both from God to humans and from Jesus to his disciples – is, 'Don't be afraid'. Here is a story from one of the four eyewitness accounts of Jesus' life (from Mark's Gospel).

That day when evening came, he said to his disciples, 'Let us go over to the other side.' Leaving the crowd behind, they took him along, just as he was, in the boat.

There were also other boats with him. A furious squall came up, and the waves broke over the boat, so that it was nearly swamped. Jesus was in the stern, sleeping on a cushion. The disciples woke him and said to him, 'Teacher, don't you care if we drown?'

He got up, rebuked the wind and said to the waves, 'Quiet! Be still!' Then the wind died down and it was completely calm.

He said to his disciples, 'Why are you so afraid? Do you still have no faith?'

They were terrified and asked each other, 'Who is this? Even the wind and the waves obey him!'

Jesus deliberately goes to sleep while a huge storm threatens to sink the boat. The storm arises out of nothing. He puts his followers in harm's way. The disciples' immediate reaction is one of complete terror.

Loss of control

Fear, as a writer called Max Lucado points out as he comments on this passage from Mark's Gospel, turns us into control freaks.[1] He is surely right to say that fear is, at least in part, about a perceived loss of control. For someone like me, who – up until cancer – had been very successful at work and enjoyed making decisions and giving orders (with varying success), one of the hardest things to come to terms with is that you are not in control. Or, to be more precise, you finally realise that you were not in control all along.

When there is fear like that of the disciples – who rudely and abruptly say to Jesus, 'Don't you care if we drown?' – the temptation is to doubt God's character, or his existence. But, in fact, God meets us most of all in the storms of life.

Lucado points out that we expect to find God, if he exists, 'in peaceful hymns … or quiet retreats … in meditations … We never expect to see him in a storm. But it's in storms that he does his finest work, for it is in storms that he has our keenest attention.'

Trust and awe

What God has been trying to teach me, I believe, is to trust him. The answer to my fear is more 'fear' – or maybe better put, 'awe'. Awe in the presence of God. Awe that I can communicate with the maker of the universe. God can appear to be asleep, or non-existent. But if you cry out to him for help – as the disciples did, however roughly and desperately – I am convinced that he will answer you.

The Bible has some amazing promises about this. For example, 'You will seek me and find me when you seek me with all your heart.' God, we are promised, doesn't play hide and seek – he wants everyone everywhere to seek him, find him and know him.

I have found this to be true. In depths of despair with cancer, when I cried to God to help, I found that he answered me. Not to cure me – although he could do that if he wants – but to reassure me that he is there, that he is in control and that he is working his purposes out.

Someone told me recently that God promises us health. I can confirm that this isn't true. But what is true is that he offers us something much more important than health. He offers us himself.

What's your worldview?

For me, and others who believe in God, the key question is: 'Do you trust God in your suffering and trouble?' But, of course, if you don't believe in God, there is an alternative worldview. You may feel that this sounds harsh – but, without God, the only alternative is to accept that life is simply a matter of randomness. Richard Dawkins is well known for that view: 'DNA neither cares nor knows. DNA just is. And we dance to its music.'[2] And this: 'Evolution has no long-term goal. There is no long-distance target, no final perfection to serve as a criterion for selection, although human vanity cherishes the absurd notion that our species is the final goal of evolution.'[3]

Is Dawkins really right that life is simply utter futility and randomness? That is not how most of us live.

Why me?

'Why me?' is a question that many of us ask. If life is random, why do we ask it? But we do – and it is a question which I have often asked myself. When I was diagnosed, it was my first reaction. It occurred to me most urgently when I was in chemotherapy in 2016 and I lost the sight in both eyes. I could hardly even see enough to walk anywhere without crashing into something. It was truly terrifying, especially the thought that perhaps the right eye, like the left, would be irreparable and I would be both blind and with (what I thought at the time) was terminal cancer.

Again I asked God the question: 'Why me?'

By the way, asking God questions is very much encouraged in the Bible. God meets us in our doubts and perplexities. He can cope with our emotions.

God allows suffering to happen for reasons that I don't fully understand. But I believe there are some reasons that can be helpful. They only give me a partial answer – but a partial answer is better than none.

A bigger story

Perhaps the most important answer I've found, as I think things through, is that I am part of a much bigger story. God is infinitely big and has eternal purposes which he is working out. I, like most of us, have a big ego and I tend to think it's all about me. I am convinced that God has allowed cancer to happen to me for his own reasons which I don't understand at the moment. But I am also convinced that when I meet God face to face, everything will fall into place and I will see how he used me (and all his children) for his own glory.

That's why trusting God is the key quality that I need when faced with fear: something very big is going on and I must place my hand into my Father's hand and go where he wants me to go.

Hobbit-like?

I love Tolkien and there is a great quote from him that I have found inspiring. At the end of *The Hobbit*, Gandalf says to Bilbo, 'You don't really suppose, do you, that all your adventures and escapes were managed by mere luck, just for your sole benefit?'[4]

The hobbits in the story are us – they are small, stupid, childish, insignificant and ignored: in fact, they are basically foolish and even laughable. Yet they are the chosen instrument of 'providence' to defeat evil. The childlike hobbits do something which the powerful ones – such as Gandalf, Aragorn and Elrond – cannot do.

Not only does this reflect on the mysterious nature of God's purposes, but it also invites the reader, I suggest, to make similar choices to that of the hobbits. In the safety of the Shire, there appears to be a 'broad way' of comfort and avoidance of difficult decisions or a 'narrow way' which is perilous. Each of us must choose – and each of our choices has moral consequences.

Each of us finds ourselves in a strange and, at times, frightening place. Often, like me, we didn't even choose that path. We found ourselves thrust onto it with no say whatsoever. In that place, we must confront the evil without and the evil within. We feel afraid, hopeless and inadequate and that we can't do what we should. I struggle every day with this. Gollum-like, I want to do good but I can't. Yet crucially, there is something much bigger (and, yes, redemptive) going on, in which we are all summoned to play a small role.

Something bigger

I think, ultimately, this sense of something 'bigger' at work is helpful. For we are all basically selfish – at least, I know that I am. We tend to think about ourselves and our own small interests and trivial preoccupations. The Bible says, 'The fear of the Lord is the beginning of wisdom.' It is this sense of something 'other' – a bigger, divine redemptive plan and a struggle against evil in which we are asked to serve – which calls to us, as to the hobbits. I suggest that this call is to place our hand in the Father's hand – the hand of the creator, who made the whole universe. That hand of God is searching for us even when we don't know it, even when – like me – we are blundering about in the dark, blind.

It's not ultimately about whether we are searching for God (good as that is to do), but about God searching for us as we wander blindly and in pain and alone in a world of sin, cancer and death. A man called Isaiah who wrote about 700 years before Christ, says of God, 'I revealed myself to those who did not ask for me; I was found by those who did not seek me.' God does not play hide and seek and he doesn't want anyone to be lost and separated from him. Of course, there is the question, 'Does God exist?' – but, even more importantly, there is the question: 'If he exists, can we trust him?' Does he have our best interests at heart?

Why anyone?
A very good question which is very linked to 'Why me?' is what we might call, 'Why anyone?' Some people drop down dead in a few minutes, others are murdered, others die tragically in senseless accidents. Small children are horrifically abused. People die senseless deaths. Why does God allow such suffering?

I don't have a ready answer for that. I don't know and I don't want to be glib. Ultimately, although the Bible gives us hints, it doesn't really answer the age-old conundrum as to why God allows evil in the first place. This is a profound and very painful question and I don't know the answer: or at least I know some theological points but I am not sure how helpful they will be to you.

But this I do know: that God doesn't leave us in the total mess we are in but cares enough about our suffering and brokenness to become human. More than that, he cares enough to experience real, physical death and go through suffering far worse than anything anyone of us will ever know.

God's answer in Jesus Christ

God's answer to suffering and pain is not theological truths, useful though they can be, but the humanity, death and resurrection of Jesus Christ. This means that, if we are Christ's, we are never alone. I have found that cancer treatment can be very lonely; sitting around for hours on uncomfortable chairs in rather dull waiting rooms. Waiting, waiting, for everything. (It may be good for me to learn some patience – impatience being one of my many faults.)

But God's promise to us, if we are his children, is that we are never truly alone, because he says to us: 'I will never leave you or forsake you.' We can be sure of that because his promises cannot be broken. And more than that, he knows what it's like.

Dr Gillian Straine in her excellent book, *Cancer: A Pilgrim Companion*, takes us to Christ in his suffering and resurrection.[5] She says this:

> *Christians believe that Christ is with us today in whatever happens to us because of what he went through on Good Friday and the resurrection ... Christ [is both] God and 'a man of suffering acquainted with infirmity'... so whatever pain we need to deal with, when we are met with our own [suffering] then we are assured of God's presence and can be certain that our suffering is held within the heart of God. 'In the hour of fear: I will put my trust in you' (Psalm 56:3).*

> *... the cross shows there is meaning in the suffering ... Because of the cross, through the cross and in the faith of what happened on the cross we have that firm ground necessary to fling that question ['Why me?']*

> *to the heavens knowing that Jesus has been*
> *there too … God says 'see I have inscribed*
> *you on the palms of my hands'.*

To this, I would add that these are palms that as we see them we see are deeply scarred. Why? For the love that Jesus had for us.

Communication

One of the main challenges of cancer, in my experience, is communication. This is true both in terms of the oncologist communicating to me, and me communicating with my family and friends. For example, just recently, the oncologist gave me a complex message when we met to review the scan that had been taken at the end of the chemotherapy. He explained that the radiologist was worried that the tumours had grown but that, when he reviewed it, he didn't think they actually had – though it was hard to be completely sure. We then spent a few minutes happily rotating the images and trying to measure them. In the end, we decided to have another scan six weeks later to be safe. Measuring tumours is relatively inexact, I have found out.

Over the next few hours, as I went around the 'Wildlife Photographer of the Year' exhibition at the nearby Natural History Museum with my wife and two friends, I chewed over the messages from the doctor. It's very helpful to have my wife along for the ride as I can check back with her. I'm quite a 'glass half full' sort of a chap. I value her medical training and calmness and it's very useful to be able to say, 'Did I miss something? What exactly did he say?'

Telling loved ones

But, even with her expertise (plus that of my sister Debs who is also medically trained), I've still found it very hard to figure out when and how much to tell everyone my latest news. Perhaps the single most difficult thing about cancer is having to pass on bad news to those closest to you, the ones you love. When I was told in 2015 that I had 18 months to live, I dreaded having to tell my three children who were then 21, 19 and 15. As our youngest was in the middle of his GCSEs and then immediately after had his 16th birthday, we decided to wait a few weeks until the day after his birthday. I can remember taking him to watch cricket at the Oval: T20 Surrey vs Kent. He was so happy and enjoying himself, while I was dreading having to tell him the next morning.

The next day, I did tell him and I also told his sister. Then we went to see our older son who was at university in Lancaster. We'd arranged a kind of macabre 'magical mystery tour' the length and breadth of the UK. We had arranged to meet my other son at the house of one of my sisters. Another sister (I have three) was also helpfully staying. We planned to go on to see my third sister near London and, finally, my mother. It was really awful to know that we had such bad news to communicate and that we were going to have to upset those we loved. As my mother said later, 'There was I [before you told me], walking up the road without a care in the world.' Then she said, which touched me greatly, 'Oh, I wish it was me.'

Flashes of humour

Everywhere we went that day, we spread gloom, sadness and tears – though sometimes a flash of humour lightened the darkness. I think it was C.S. Lewis who described humour as God's gift to humanity to make sense of a broken world. In my case, this was our older son – who was expecting his parents but not his whole family – saying that he thought since we were all coming it must be to tell us that the dog had died!

The same son had also provided some much-needed light relief three years earlier when I was first diagnosed with cancer. I wanted to tell him but, as chance would have it, he had a Taiwanese exchange student staying with us that week and, being hospitable, our son was hard to get away from his guest. Eventually, in desperation, I invented a story to get him on his own, saying, 'I've got a problem with my iPad, could you come next door and give me a hand?' Finally, having him on his own in a separate room, I told him about my cancer and then asked him if he had any questions. 'So there's nothing wrong with your iPad?', he replied!

All of the above illustrates the difficulties and pain of having to communicate about cancer. Cancer is the great disrupter – changing, complicating and sometimes even breaking relationships. Cancer (and death in general) is awful not only because it makes communication difficult and painful, but because, ultimately, it will end communication completely. There is no voice from beyond the grave, despite desperate searches by poor misguided people making frantic efforts using Ouija boards and séances.

A voice from beyond the grave

That sense of desperate desire for communication, for a voice from the dead, is well captured by Eddie Izzard, the transvestite comedian in a recent article:

'Towards the end of the film [Believe: The Eddie Izzard Story], *I started talking about my mother…' he recalls. 'And I said something revelatory: "I know why I'm doing all this," I said. "Everything I do in life is trying to get her back. I think if I do enough things… that maybe she'll come back." When he said those words, he says, it felt like his unconscious speaking. The thought stayed with him that 'I do believe I started performing and doing all sorts of big, crazy, ambitious things because on some level, on some childlike magical-thinking level, I thought doing those things might bring her back.'*

'… I have a very strong sense that we are only on this planet for a short length of time,' he says. 'And that is only growing. Religious people might think it goes on after

death. My feeling is that if that is the case it would be nice if just one person came back and let us know it was all fine, all confirmed. Of all the billions of people who have died, if just one of them could come through the clouds and say, you know, "It's me Jeanine, it's brilliant, there's a really good spa", that would be great.'[6]

Dear Eddie, Dear Reader, this is exactly the Christian claim: that of all the billions of people who have died, one indeed did come back. To be more specific, he not only came back but he invites us to hear him today: that death itself is not the end.

Has anyone come back?

Not many of us will doubt the historical existence of Jesus Christ. No serious historian would – there is too much evidence. Not many of us will question that Jesus died the death of a common criminal on a basic, wooden cross in first-century Palestine and that his dead body was put into a sealed stone tomb. Most of us will be familiar with the claim that Jesus came back to life several days later – a claim not of revival from unconsciousness but of genuine resurrection. One day utterly dead; three days later, utterly alive. Could that possibly be true?

If that claim is not true, you can get rid of 99.99% of Christianity. Some of the Christian morals (being kind, honest, etc.) may make people nicer to live with – but that's it. And, actually, if the resurrection isn't true, Christianity is deceptive – because it is totally founded on the claim that Jesus rose from the dead.

However, just let's consider the possibility that it *is* true. (And there really are only two options here – either Jesus stayed dead, or he rose from death to life.) If the resurrection *is* true, then someone *has* come back. He has shown us that life after death is possible. He even tells us what life after death can be like.[7]

So Jesus is a type of 'front runner'. He leads the way. He shows us what's possible. But, more than that, he demonstrates that he is stronger than our greatest enemy: death. Death could not hold Jesus Christ in the grave. If that is true – and I believe it is utterly true – that is truly wonderful news.

What is death?

I was struck reading a book by J.C. Ryle, the first

Bishop of Liverpool. Christians, he said, believe that death is not the end. It is solemn and troubling – but it does not need to be regarded with terror. We do not need to fear death if we trust in Jesus Christ.

For the Christian, death has lost its sting. Because of Jesus' resurrection, those who trust Christ have nothing to fear for our bodies in death, for they will be changed: we will rise again, wonderfully remade in the image of the Lord. All of the pains and suffering of life will be gone. The grave itself is defeated. So with us: all will hear the voice of Jesus at the end of all things and all will be called out of the grave.

To a non-believer who rejected that voice when alive, the voice of Jesus at the end of all things, commanding them to come out, will be a terrible thing. But today, the voice of Jesus, which has power over death itself, invites us – indeed implores us – to come to him, rather than condemning us to go from him.

The offer
Now is the time to receive the free offer which the voice of Jesus lays before us – the offer of eternal life and a living friendship with God. Who would not want to be a friend of God? Who would

not want to defeat death? Who would not want eternal life?

As we face death as Christians we can say, very boldly, with God's help, 'In peace I will lie down and sleep, for you alone, Lord, make me dwell in safety.'

'I wish I had your faith'

One of the most common comments people make to me is something along the lines of, 'you are an inspiration' or 'your faith is amazing' or 'I wish I had your faith'.

Sometimes they put the same feeling in a slightly different way, such as: 'I am not a religious person' ('unlike you', being the implication – and possibly, 'let's stop talking about it' being another). Please, I really want to stress to everyone reading this, this story is not about me or my faith. I am not a naturally resilient person, or a 'religious' or 'spiritual' one. I am probably not very different from you. It is not about me. It is about Jesus Christ – the one who has powerfully helped me, who is available to all, available without charge and without discrimination.

The journey of life

Apart from the last seven years, I can't remember a single time that I have been treated in a hospital in my whole life, except for sports injuries. When I was well, I never went to a hospital except to visit sick friends and relatives. Why would you? It is hardly a place for a casual visit. Cancer hospitals are, with the best will in the world, grim places.

Without warning, cancer suddenly meant that I was in a hospital all the time – sometimes two. I had one for my eyes (St Thomas') and one for cancer (the Royal Marsden). If you read about hospitals being overloaded, I feel I am probably personally responsible!

Before being diagnosed with cancer, life was like being on a trainline with the (interim) destination marked as 'Comfortable Retirement: Arrival 2028'. (Although, of course, that's not the ultimate destination – but we don't want to think about that.) The train of life for many of us (not for all, I realise, but for many) is familiar and comfortable. (Again, I know I am very fortunate.) For the lucky ones, things are predictable and life is pleasant.

Suddenly, without any warning, on my train journey, there was a brutal 'jolt' and everything suddenly changed. Abruptly, I found myself being shunted across to a new and unfamiliar 'line' with a new (and, this time, final) destination marked as 'Death: Arrival 2016'. All the familiar landmarks as I looked out the window of my 'train' had changed irretrievably and forever – work, holidays and pleasure turned into scans, chemotherapy and surgery.

Cancer is like being shoved into a parallel universe; once you are in it, you can't get back to normality. Even if, like me, you learn for a while to live with cancer, the Grim Reaper has joined the train and moved into your carriage and is sitting opposite you, regarding you with a cold eye.

The oncologist

For me, part of this process of adjusting to a new 'trainline' has been getting to know my oncologist who, in my case, is a doctor called Robin Jones. Robin is an absolutely amazing oncologist: he's a world expert on sarcomas and is often travelling and speaking at conferences throughout the world. He is also an incredibly kind and compassionate doctor, for whom nothing is too much trouble, and he is someone who you feel really cares about his patients. His 'bedside manner' is amazing –

and I know this is sadly untypical of some people's experience with oncologists.

Over time, through experience and also through looking at the evidence of his impressive track record, I have come to completely trust and respect Robin. If he suggests I do something, then I will do it. Sometimes, for example, he says, 'Let's wait a couple of months and see what happens.' Sometimes he says, 'Now we need to resort to treatment.' I trust him completely.

When it was eventually decided that my second type of cancer was different from the first type – not a sarcoma but non-pulmonary small cell lung carcinoma – Robin said, 'Well, I should really move you on to a lung cancer specialist now.' Fortunately, I persuaded him to keep me on, pointing out that maybe some variety from only doing sarcomas is good for him! The reason I did that is that I both trust and like Robin. I trusted him for his expertise and I felt we had built a good relationship over many years.

I realise that he's doing his best with a difficult-to-treat disease and that, of course, there is no guarantee that the treatment will keep working. But I trust him. In fact, you could say I believe in him.

The Divine Oncologist

In the same way as Robin, my 'earthly physician', is key for me – Jesus Christ, the 'heavenly physician' – is even more central. It's exactly the same except Robin, as far as I know, can't raise people from the dead (although that would be a very useful skill for an oncologist).

When you initially get cancer, people suggest all kinds of remedies. Some of them are quite strange – like eating only radishes. Actually, eating healthily is a good thing and I do like radishes – but not as a sole dietary intake. I have a friendly nutritionist, Nancy, in America, who recommended all kinds of healthy food to eat, natural minerals and vitamins which I take daily. But some people I have met and spoken to say, 'Don't even go to the doctor, just eat differently.' Often these schemes are hare-brained: I read a sad story about a lady who was a captain in the British Army and went to America to eat a very specific diet and who spent a huge amount on the treatment – all to no avail.

The BBC had a sad article about a lady called Gemma Nuttall whose family raised thousands of pounds when she was diagnosed with terminal cancer and given months to live.[8] Her mother tells the story of how the family gave everything they had, even selling their house, to send their daughter to a German clinic which specialises in alternative treatments. They raised a lot of money from strangers, including the actress, Kate Winslet. The article pointed out that the benefit of such clinics is questionable, and that the bills are enormous – one visit alone cost £93,000.

The article touched me as, of course, I have been living with an incurable cancer diagnosis for the last four years and many people have recommended similar treatment to me.

The best treatment?

How should we think about this? We must surely have deep compassion for these poor, desperate people. I immediately thought of the sad and lonely woman in the Bible who had 'spent all she had' on medical treatment and who timidly touched Jesus in the hope of being healed. No doubt there were expensive cures and clinics in AD 30 with dubious outcomes. She seems to have tried them all.

Eventually, she went to Jesus. She was afraid and embarrassed about her illness. She secretly crept up to Jesus while he was walking in a large crowd and reached out and touched him. Immediately, she was healed and Jesus turned around as he felt the power go out of him. The Lord is so kind to the sick and to those facing death. I long for my suffering friends to know that God has entered this sad, fallen, sinful world and he meets us right in the midst of our grief and sorrow.

What we can offer – as well as compassion to those suffering from cancer or other terminal diseases – is the one thing that the world craves above all things: hope in the face of death. I love to tell people how the Lord has, by his death, defeated death.

God's treatment

God's ultimate 'treatment' is not a philosophy or theology or morality – but a person. When nothing else makes sense, and nothing else is left, Jesus is there and he will hold us fast: if we will only trust in him.

Some of the self-help treatments surrounding cancer – whether in terms of mental or physical therapies – certainly have their place. But, in the final analysis, what we would hope for all those with cancer is that they had access to a top oncologist at a top hospital. Likewise, the best (and, in fact, only) place to fix our problem of sin and our broken relationship with God is Jesus Christ.

I trust Jesus because of the evidence I have. That evidence is primarily in the four eyewitness accounts about his life (which Christians call 'gospels' and which, appropriately enough, means 'good news'). Added to that first-century eyewitness evidence is my personal experience that God can deliver what he promises. I trust that God has my best interests at heart, that he is in control of everything, and that I need to be 'treated' by him.

It's because I know that I need God's help that I go to him for 'treatment' for the things that are wrong in my life. I know I can't get rid of my sin and selfishness myself – no matter how much I try.

Jesus – the ultimate doctor

Jesus himself used the terminology of doctors and treatment when he was criticised for associating with people whom respectable society viewed as beyond the pale.

Here is how one contemporary account describes it:

> *While Jesus was having dinner at Levi's*
> *house, many tax collectors and sinners*
> *were eating with him and his disciples, for*
> *there were many who followed him. When*
> *the teachers of the law who were Pharisees*
> *saw him eating with the sinners and tax*
> *collectors, they asked his disciples: 'Why*
> *does he eat with tax collectors and sinners?'*
> *On hearing this, Jesus said to them, 'It is*
> *not the healthy who need a doctor, but the*
> *sick. I have not come to call the righteous,*
> *but sinners.'*

The Pharisees were the very religious people of Jesus' day. They thought that God loved them because they were so keen on religion, and they hated people like Levi who were tax collectors. Tax collectors have probably never been the most popular people. They were particularly detested in first-century Palestine because they were the agents of the hated Roman occupiers. But Jesus points out the paradox – the religious don't think they need 'treatment' because they are healthy, while the outcasts of society accept that they do need to see a doctor.

Meeting Jesus

To meet Jesus, we must first realise we *need* to meet him. When life is, on balance, full of joy and happiness, we think about anything apart from death – even though, of course, it is the ultimate destination of the journey for everyone without exception.

The French philosopher and mathematician Blaise Pascal said: 'Being unable to cure death, wretchedness and ignorance, men have decided, in order to be happy, not to think about such things.'

When I think of my life before I had cancer (and I was a Christian then), I can now see that I was focusing much of my thoughts, energies and time on things that ultimately don't matter. Nobody on their deathbed says, 'I wish I had spent more time in the office'. Or as Dr Johnson famously said, 'Depend upon it, sir, when a man knows he is to be hanged in a fortnight, it concentrates his mind wonderfully.'

Isn't it the same for us? We avoid thinking of our death at all costs because we think it's so far off. My prognosis of 18 months concentrated my mind wonderfully. But whether it's a fortnight, 18 months, or 40 years, death is waiting for us all.

Reactions to cancer

There are various reactions to cancer or any serious illness. My family, friends and contacts have been very sympathetic and caring. Many people say things to me like 'bad luck' or 'stay strong' and I understand why they say that. Any encouragement is welcome. When I was first diagnosed, I remember a friend who is a convinced atheist telling me, 'I gave God a surprise today: I popped into a church to say a prayer for you.' I was very touched by that and, indeed, by the feeling of love and outpouring of support from many people.

Cancer can be very lonely and the constant support, especially from my immediate family, is amazing. Special mention to my wife, Jeanette, who has sat alongside me for almost all the treatments on the rather uncomfortable chairs which the Marsden provides. The patients themselves get nice padded chairs! While my cancer has its challenges – for example, the way life goes 'on hold' and it's so very difficult to plan anything – I can also continue to enjoy life. I don't have a 'bucket list' *per se*, but I do love to spend time with my family and family holidays especially are an absolute pleasure which I truly anticipate with great eagerness.

I also enjoy (saddo that I am) going to see my beloved Watford FC. Some of my friends might think this is a particularly refined form of suffering – though strangely enough, from the precise moment I was diagnosed with incurable cancer in 2015, Watford have had pretty much the best run in their history, or at least equal to the early 1980s under the late, great Graham Taylor. Make of that what you will. It's great fun going to home or away matches with various family members: it's the shared experience that makes it so memorable, especially on the rare occasion that the Mighty Hornets win.

Acknowledging the diagnosis

I hope I try not to be obsessed with cancer, but it is hard to avoid thinking about it every day. Of course, I had it for quite a while before I knew it. So, the first step for me, though shocking, was to be aware that there was a problem that needed treatment.

It's the same with our relationship with God: the first step back towards him is the realisation that we are sick – that we need to visit his 'hospital' to get right with him. We may deny that we are spiritually ill but, in reality, it's obvious that we are sick when we look at the inevitability of our death.

Jesus Christ is the ultimate 'oncologist of death'. He has both the power and the compassion to help us. He can and will help us in our 'illness'.

Jesus' compassion and power

One of the four gospel writers was a man called Luke. Uniquely in the Bible, he was a Gentile, not a Jew; he was also a doctor, so he was very interested in medical issues. Time and time again in Luke's account, we see Jesus' compassion and his healing power. Often it's revealed in the smallest details, such as the story of a bereaved widow in a place called Nain, which is a small town in Galilee, in the north of Palestine. Let me tell you about it.

Travelling to Nain one day with his disciples, Jesus is about to enter the town when he and his followers meet a funeral procession coming the other way. It's a burial procession for a young boy; his body is being followed by a crowd, headed by his weeping mother, a widow. Jesus then does something very surprising: he touches the bier on which the dead boy is being carried out of the town to his burial.

According to Jewish law, touching the dead makes the person unclean. Death, as it were, corrupts everyone who comes into contact with it. No normal rabbi would do that. But Jesus' contact with death has precisely the opposite effect – by touching the bier and then commanding the boy to get up, Jesus reverses the power of death. The boy comes back from the dead and Jesus gives him back to his mother.

Here in this story, Jesus shows both compassion and power. It's the combination of the two together that's the key. We might imagine a remote infinite Divinity who sees us suffering from cancer and could do something if he wanted to, but has no motive for doing so. Or we might imagine a compassionate human – our father or mother, for example, if we were a sick child with cancer – who cares deeply about us but who can't do anything to help.

But Jesus has both characteristics. He is deeply moved by the predicament of this poor woman and her dead son – literally, in the Greek in which the gospel is written, 'his intestines are twisted'. But, equally, he is able to say one word, bringing the boy back from the dead and healing him from whatever disease killed him in the first place.

Why did Jesus die?

Jesus' identification with our death-haunted human condition goes far beyond this. Just shortly after meeting this widow, Jesus himself is also going to die. The death of Jesus is a truly staggering, almost inconceivable, fact. To believe that the God who made and controls the entire universe became human and experienced death on our behalf is astonishing. Not a death surrounded by health professionals doing all they could to ease his passing, but death surrounded by professional torturers doing all they could to make it as painful as possible. What was his goal? To rescue us; to heal us. What was his motive? His love for us.

This love is not because we are inherently loveable. It is not because, for example, we are naturally friends with God, and he wants to help us, as anyone would help a friend. On the contrary. I am by nature a rebel against God. I don't want him telling me what to do. Naturally speaking, I want to do what I like. One of my friends is honest enough to admit that this is one of his main reasons for rejecting Christianity.

Rebels – really?

And it's our root problem: we are rebels against

God and, every day, we tell him to 'get lost' – maybe overtly, or maybe simply by ignoring him. We live in a broken world, and each of us is partly responsible for that brokenness. The amazing message of the Christian faith is this: that while, by nature, we are rebels against God, God came into the world as a human being and died on a cross for us. He did this not while we were his friends, but while we were his enemies; not while we loved him, but while we hated him. The message streaming from the cross is the offer from God of forgiveness for the evil that each one of us has within us – what the Bible calls our 'sin'.

But each one of us is, by nature, a rebel: we want our own way, we want to be our own boss. 'Go away God,' we say, shaking our fist at him (or possibly rather quietly), 'I am the Master of my fate, I am the Captain of my soul.' We rebel against the Father – but he offers us a way back to him through his Son's death. Ultimately, if we reject that offer, then we will have to live with the ultimate consequence of our sin – which is what the Bible calls 'the second death': eternal separation from God.

Does that sound harsh? But how could a perfect God let people who are selfish and proud into his perfect heaven? We would spoil it immediately. We may not be as bad as others we can think of – but few of us would be so crass as to claim to be completely perfect. When Jesus (the perfect, sinless one) died on the cross, he paid the penalty for all the ways in which we (the far from perfect ones) have rebelled against our creator. He acted as a substitute; dying in our place. The perfect and sinless one experienced and defeated death so that we who are broken and sinful can triumph over death through him.

Dear Reader, I urge you to consider this. We are all on 'the way to dusty death', as the saying goes. As you read these words, Jesus is, as it were, 'touching the bier' which is carrying you to death. The question is: what will you do?

What will you do?
I have felt so powerfully that 'touch of my bier', that presence of the Lord Jesus since I have been ill. I have felt him standing by my side at the point of surgery and treatment. As I have been wheeled down to the surgery, I feel him there alongside, saying, 'I will never leave you or forsake you.' Wouldn't you want the divine oncologist by your side, on your team, rooting

for you? He speaks to us on our bier: do we want to defeat death or not?

How do we respond to that touch? Coming to faith in Jesus is not about being good, or being religious, or understanding theological systems. It's certainly not about gaining insight into 'how to understand suffering'. As the widow of Nain found in her grief and sadness, it's about realising that we need help, that we need to meet God face to face, know him personally, and have a relationship with him.

Our biggest problem?

When we receive a terminal diagnosis, imminent death presents itself as a monstrous problem. But our biggest problem is not death – but the fact that our relationship with God is broken, damaged beyond human repair by all the things we have done wrong. We need to get back to God.

That is our deepest need – and a longing that God has put in everyone's soul. A teacher and writer called Augustine who lived around 400 years after Christ said: 'You have made us for yourself, O Lord, and our heart is restless until it rests in you.'

Is there a God?

If you are not sure there even is a God, I suggest you ask a Christian friend (I hope you have one) to read one of the four eyewitness accounts of Jesus' life with you and chat it through. I do that a lot with friends, using John's gospel and some notes. There is an excellent resource which I have loved sharing in the last four years: *The Word One to One*, which is simply John's gospel plus some questions and answers.[9] I am not asking you to take a leap in the dark but inviting you to 'kick the tyres' or 'try before you buy'. Is it true? Is there a God? Please, I beg you, look at the evidence.

We can also ask God for help. The prayer, 'God if you are there, show yourself to me', is a powerful one, if prayed genuinely. After all, what have you to lose? If there is nothing there, you have lost nothing. But I am utterly convinced there is a creator God who made the universe, who is there and who will answer you. How? Primarily through his word, the Bible, but God may choose other means.

A friend of mine became a Christian when, one night, he saw the words in his bedroom: 'Jesus Christ is the Son of God'. That's very unusual (I have never had such a dramatic experience) but

God speaks to us in one way or another. Whether we will listen to him is another question.

A spiritual power cut

Imagine you are in a giant library with thousands of books. Everything in this library is illuminated by powerful lights in the ceiling. Suddenly, there is a power cut and you are in an immense darkness. Then and only then, you see that golden light is pouring out of one book which is shining brightly, like a star. The power cut has made everything dark – and that is the only reason that the brilliant light from the book can be seen. It may be that God uses the suffering in our lives as a 'power cut' so that we can see the light of life shining out of his word.

In cancer, I can do nothing. For control freaks like me, that is a shock. All I can do is passively take the medicine. I just sit there for hours and hours with chemotherapy. Or lie there unconscious while the surgeon cuts away. This is the type of 'eternal life' medicine I recommend. When it comes to eternal life, there is nothing I can do. I just take the medicine and it heals me. I contribute nothing to it, other than watching it like a chemotherapy drug infusing into my bloodstream.

The medicine of eternity

What does the label on the medicine promise? In John's gospel, it says:

> *Then Jesus declared, 'I am the bread of life. Whoever comes to me will never go hungry, and whoever believes in me will never be thirsty. But as I told you, you have seen me and still, you do not believe. All those the Father gives me will come to me, and whoever comes to me I will never drive away. For I have come down from heaven not to do my will but to do the will of him who sent me. And this is the will of him who sent me, that I shall lose none of all those he has given me, but raise them up at the last day. For my Father's will is that everyone who looks to the Son and believes in him shall have eternal life, and I will raise them up at the last day.'*

What does it mean to 'come' to Jesus Christ? J.C. Ryle said this: 'It means that movement of the soul when someone, feeling their sins, finding out they cannot save themselves, hears of Christ, applies to Christ, trusts in Christ, lays hold of Christ, leans all his weight on Christ for salvation.'[10]

When Ryle talks about 'feeling our sins', he means sensing and knowing that our relationship with God is broken. If we can fix that, everything else is fixed: including cancer and even death. If we *can't* fix that, then even if we live a wonderful, problem-free and healthy life to the age of 100, we are broken and at risk of eternal separation from God: a second and worse death.

Who is it for?

Who may come to Jesus? Anyone. Anyone at all. It doesn't matter if you are the most moral person who ever lived – or the worst. It doesn't matter if you are 'very religious' or 'very unreligious'. The offer of treatment is exactly the same to all. Ironically, I often find that the person who has behaved worse in life realises that their need for treatment is the most urgent.

When I first had cancer, I didn't go to the doctor because I didn't know I had it. In the same way, the biggest danger is thinking something like 'well, I never did anyone any wrong'. Even if that's true (which I very much doubt), our biggest wrong is not against each other – but against God.

Every day, we live in his world but rebel against our Father, saying to him, 'I will do it "my way".'

Although we reject God, he doesn't yet reject us – but, today, invites any that want to come back home to him. There is no cost: we don't have to do anything, other than accept the free medicine.

What's the offer? This is it: eternal life with God. What's the alternative? It's this: eternal death, which means the ultimate separation from God.

The story of Job

Let me tell one more story from the Bible to conclude. There is a mysterious book called Job which was written many hundreds of years before Christ. Job was an immensely wealthy and holy man. Satan (the Devil) comes before God and God points out Job's devotion to him. 'No wonder,' replies Satan, 'for look at what you have given him'. God then allows the Devil to take away, first, all of Job's possessions and children and, subsequently, to inflict on him an awful disease. But the Devil is not allowed to kill him. Job sits alone, utterly bereft, on the rubbish heap. It is a sad, confusing tale.

Three friends, wise men, come to comfort Job. If you know the expression, 'Job's comforters', you will know they are worse than useless. The bulk of the book is then a poetic dialogue between Job and these three men. They say he must have been secretly sinful, otherwise, this disaster would not have happened. Job defends himself. The argument gets more and more heated before ending inconclusively. Another younger man then rebukes both the comforters and Job.

Finally, God himself speaks to Job out of a storm and says to him, 'Look Job, do you think you are like me? Can you create something from nothing?' Job humbles himself and admits, 'No, I'm not. And, no, I can't.' Job is then restored to even greater happiness and eventually, many years later, dies full of years and surrounded by a new and even larger family.

The story of Job tells us a number of things. God encourages us to be truthful with him, which means telling him exactly how we feel. Many people I know with cancer feel angry with God. Job is very angry with God and says things that, if they were not in the Bible, we would think were deeply shocking. Yet God at the end rebukes the comforters saying, 'you have not spoken the truth about me as my servant Job has.'

Bad things happen to good people

Bad things happen to 'good' people for reasons that we ultimately cannot understand this side of meeting God face to face. Being a Christian is not an insurance policy against disaster: if anything, it's perhaps the reverse. Crucially, suffering and cancer is not a sign of God's displeasure – because we are not accepted or protected by God on the basis of how good we are. This was the huge mistake both of Job's comforters and, paradoxically, of Job himself. Writer Christopher Ash points out that Job's friends argued along the lines: God is fair – you are suffering – therefore you have been bad. Job replies: I am suffering – I haven't been bad – therefore God is unfair.[11]

This feeling of God loving us because we are loveable (or hating us because we are bad) is also the biggest misunderstanding of people today about the Christian faith. Maybe we see God as some kind of 'cosmic slot machine'. We put our good deeds into the slot, and out comes God's acceptance or rejection. But it's the reverse: we are accepted by God not because we are good, but because we know we are 'sick' and can't get right with him by our own efforts.

Jesus' suffering on our behalf

Yes, bad things happen to 'good' people. Life is full of suffering. But God decided to come in human form to suffer on our behalf.

A man called Dietrich Bonhoeffer was a German pastor who opposed the Nazi persecution of the Jews. Sadly, most German Christians turned a blind eye to the Holocaust. Bonhoeffer was imprisoned in a concentration camp for his courageous stand and was executed a couple of weeks before the end of the war. In his last days, he smuggled out of the camp a piece of paper which contained the phrase 'Only a suffering God can help us.'

That's the Christian belief: that God became human and, in his humanity, suffered. He knows what it's like not because God knows everything (although he does) but because Jesus has experienced it first-hand on the cross. Jesus empathises with us and knows what we are going through – and I find that thought amazing. More than that, he has decided to do something about it.

His choice

This solidarity with us has a twist though. In one respect, his suffering is quite different from ours.

I have no choice but to suffer with my cancer – but Jesus had a choice. He could have opted out. He was tempted to do that just before his death – but he chose to stay and fight his fear and go to his death. Why? For love of the lost and suffering human beings.

This means not only that Jesus (100% God and 100% human) suffered something far worse than anything I could ever go through, but that this suffering on the cross is the 'Miracle Cure'. Not for cancer but for something worse – being separated from God for eternity.

Job's faith – at his lowest ebb

I find the story of Job so helpful because of his faith. At his lowest ebb, with absolutely nothing left and stricken by a terrible disease, and also full of anger, loneliness and doubts, Job says:

> *Oh, that my words were recorded,*
> *that they were written on a scroll,*
> *that they were inscribed with an iron*
> *tool on lead, or engraved in rock for ever!*
> *I know that my redeemer lives,*
> *and that in the end he will stand on*
> *the earth.*

And after my skin has been destroyed,
yet in my flesh I will see God;
I myself will see him
with my own eyes – I, and not another.
How my heart yearns within me!

He sees that he has a living redeemer and that this redeemer will stand on the earth. He knows that he will see him with his own eyes. When Job says that his redeemer will stand on the earth, it's literally 'on the dust', or on Job's grave. Each of us, if we believe in Jesus, will have the same privilege. Jesus will stand on our grave, or our ashes if we don't have one, and we will be remade, new and free of suffering. We will see God face to face and know him and love him and enjoy him for all eternity.

Faith in the midst of fear

None of that means it's easy. Cancer is truly a horrible and terrifying disease. As I said at the beginning and say again at the end: I am not at all an expert on living with cancer. All the Christian truths which I hold to be true don't stop me feeling afraid of cancer. Yes, I am afraid of dying. I have to be honest about that. As Woody Allen famously said, 'It's not that I'm afraid to die – I just don't want to be there when it happens.'[12]

Even though I know the destination, 'the beyond', is amazing (to be with God), the route there is grim. Thinking about death from a Christian perspective is a bit like booking a fantastic holiday in, say, the Seychelles – but having to put up with the giant mess of Heathrow Airport en route. So I have a mix of emotions.

When I recall the death of my father from cancer in 2003, I experience the same combination of feelings. My father was a pastor and had a strong Christian faith and knew where he was going. Nonetheless, when my sisters and I were at his bedside in his last hours as he was dying, it was very hard.

Death is a terrible enemy and being a Christian doesn't mean you can avoid it, even though you believe death has been beaten.

The valley of the shadow of death

Perhaps the most famous chapter in the Bible is Psalm 23 and the line, 'Even though I walk through the valley of the shadow of death, I will fear no evil, for you are with me.' God doesn't offer a bypass around that deathly valley. But he does say that when we go through it – and we all must go through it sooner or later – he will be with us.

Ah, I can anticipate some of you are thinking … That's just 'whistling in the dark', wishful thinking; Christianity is a crutch for people who are limping. I'm not limping and therefore 'Sir, I have no need of that hypothesis,' as the French scholar Laplace supposedly said to Napoleon about God. But death is an inescapable truth. The Founding Father, Benjamin Franklin, said, 'You can avoid anything in life except Death and Taxes.' Actually, events such as the 'Panama Papers' show that you can avoid tax – but not one of us can avoid death. One day, Dear Reader, like me, you will sooner or later be staring death in the face.

The Ballad of Buster Scruggs
This is well illustrated by the recent (very dark) film by the Coen Brothers, *The Ballad of Buster Scruggs*.[13] The movie consists of six 'short stories', each one getting darker and darker. *Vox*, in their review, said:

> *If you puzzle long enough, though, you realize that the theme is … that bad stuff*

*happens to good people, and when we try to
explain it, we're left just telling more stories
about bad stuff happening to good people.
The universe does not play favorites, and it
rarely makes a lot of sense; the best any of
us can do is to just keep plugging along.*[14]

But even to 'just keep plugging along' brings us,
sooner or later, to the same place. The last of the
six stories (spoiler alert) is called, appropriately
enough, 'Mortal Remains'. It has five apparent
strangers, uncomfortably jammed together in a
stagecoach on a long journey (from which they
cannot escape because the stagecoach will not
stop). As they chat, seemingly randomly, we see
that three of the five strangers have very different
philosophies. There is a trapper who is a Darwinian
and says, 'people fight like ferrets in a sack'. The
lady, who is a moralist, argues that 'there are two
types of people: sinners and good people'. The
Frenchman is a cynic who thinks it's all luck and
that even the lady's love for her husband is fake.

Soon enough, the story becomes all too clear:
the other two passengers in the stagecoach (an
Englishman and an Irishman) are 'reapers of
souls' who are taking the three unsuspecting

travellers to death, when the stagecoach stops. In each of the stories, someone is just about to die in a pointless and random way, they just don't know it yet. And none of the philosophies of life outlined is going to save the passengers – neither Darwinism nor moralism nor cynicism.

Maybe you are thinking that it sounds like a depressing movie, but that it's just a story. A dark one but a story. But as the Englishman notes sardonically to the unsuspecting trio, 'We love hearing about ourselves. As long as the people in the stories are us, but not us. Not us in the end, especially.'

One destination

But, in the end, whether we like it or not, we are all in a stagecoach heading to only one destination: death. You and I are all in the same stagecoach, it's just that some of us are nearer the destination than others.

But now, suddenly, out of nowhere, there comes to you – stuck on the stagecoach of death – an offer of a rescue, an offer of eternal life. How do we know that the offer is true? When you are in bad shape, trapped in the stagecoach, it's an appealing thought compared with the alternative.

But the question is not: is it *helpful*, but is it *true*? Is there something beyond death?

I have argued that if we trust God, he has proved that he will rescue us, stand on our graves and say to our bodies 'come out' – because he did that with his own Son. Christopher Ash points out that Charles Jennens – the librettist or 'arranger' of the words of Handel's *Messiah* – was absolutely right to join the aria 'I Know That My Redeemer Liveth' with 'For Now Is Christ Risen'. For we know that the chill power of death has been obliterated by the one who went in our place before us, and who stands ready to embrace us in his everlasting arms on the other side.[15]

If only one person came back

How do we know that the Christian faith is true? Because Jesus proved it by coming back from the dead. To Eddie Izzard's heart-rending plea, 'if only one person came back', there is an answer from Jesus the Messiah. 'Yes, I did – and here I am. Trust in me.'

This is my offer to you which I make not because I have any power or goodness at all but because I am authorised to offer it to you as a fellow sufferer. Jesus said:

*And this is the will of him who sent me,
that I shall lose none of all of those he has
given me, but raise them up at the last day.
For my Father's will is that everyone who
looks to the Son and believes in him shall
have eternal life, and I will raise him up at
the last day.*

Hope in the face of cancer and death

I tell you then with great seriousness that there is hope in the face of cancer and death. You really can have a Saviour for your life and know a 'peace which passes all understanding' – now and forever.

Despite many fears along the way, my predominant emotion is one of amazing peace and this is where I leave you: resting in the arms of my loving Saviour. 'Come,' he says to you too, 'believe in me.'

Endnotes

1. Max Lucado, *Fearless: Imagine Your Life Without Fear* (Thomas Nelson, 2012).

2. Richard Dawkins, *River Out of Eden: A Darwinian View of Life* (Basic Books, 1995).

3. Richard Dawkins, *The Blind Watchmaker: Why the Evidence of Evolution Reveals a Universe Without Design* (Norton & Co, 1986).

4. J.R.R. Tolkien, *The Hobbit* (George Allen & Unwin, 1937).

5. Gillian Straine, *Cancer: A Pilgrim Companion* (SPCK, 2017).

6. Tim Adams, "Eddie Izzard: 'Everything I do in life is trying to get my mother back'", *The Guardian*, 10 September 2017.

7. John 14:2

8. "We chose cancer crowdfunding over making memories", *BBC*, 6 March 2019.

9. William Taylor and Richard Borgonon, *The Word One to One* (10Publishing, 2013), www.theword121.com.

10. J.C. Ryle, *Expository Thoughts on John* (Banner of Truth, 1987).

11. Christopher Ash, *Job: Out of the Storm* (IVP, 2009).

12. Woody Allen, quoted in Fred Metcalf, *Penguin Dictionary of Modern Humorous Quotations* (Penguin, 2001).

13. *The Ballad of Buster Scruggs* (2018), dir. Ethan Coen and Joel Coen.

14. Alissa Wilkinson, "Netflix's *Ballad of Buster Scruggs* is an old West folk tale, with a signature Coen brothers twist", *Vox*, 16 November 2018.

15. Ash, *Job: Out of the Storm.*

a division of **10** **ofthose**.com

10Publishing is the publishing house of **10ofThose**. It is committed to producing quality Christian resources that are biblical and accessible.

www.10ofthose.com is our online retail arm selling thousands of quality books at discounted prices.

For information contact: **info@10ofthose.com** or check out our website: **www.10ofthose.com**